JAPANE

A History from Beginning to End

Copyright © 2023 by Hourly History.

All rights reserved.

Table of Contents

Introduction
The Meiji Restoration
War with China and the Annexation of Korea
The Japanese Empire during World War I
Kōdōha: Rise of Militarism and Nationalism
Manchuria and the Kwantung Army
Coups and Political Violence
Alliance with Germany and Italy
World War II: Pearl Harbor
The Tide Turns
End of the Empire
Conclusion
Bibliography

Introduction

In 1603, Japan entered the Edo period, a time when the country was ruled not by emperors but by a series of *shōguns*—military dictators from the Tokugawa clan. There were still emperors, but their role became largely ceremonial, and they had little direct influence over the way in which the country was run. While this period of rule by a single house, known as the Tokugawa Shogunate, brought stability after a long period of warfare, it also brought stagnation as Japanese society reverted to a basically feudal model where the shōgun enforced his rule through the warrior class, the *samurai*.

Contact and trade with other nations were minimized. In fact, the only foreign trade permitted during the Edo period was carried out with China and the Dutch through the port of Nagasaki. Christianity, which had arrived in Japan with early traders from Europe, was also almost completely crushed. Japanese society remained rooted in the ideals of the medieval world, where the farmer was held up as the ideal person. However, as the population of Japan grew, it became more and more difficult to produce sufficient food and distribute it effectively to all parts of Japan. By the time of the first known national census in 1721, there were at least 25 million commoners in Japan, ruled by over 4 million samurai. A refusal to adopt ideas of commerciality and advances in technology and agriculture led to a series of famines that culminated in the Great Tenmei famine in 1782, which may have led to the deaths of up to one million people.

Then, in 1853, a formation of American warships appeared off the coast of Japan. This was a flotilla of the U.S. Navy under the command of Commodore Matthew C. Perry, and its mission was simple: to persuade Japan to begin trading with the United States, using force if necessary. Without a modern navy of its own, the Tokugawa Shogunate was compelled in 1854 to agree to a humiliating treaty with the U.S. called the Kanagawa Treaty, also known as the Treaty of Peace and Amity. This treaty forced Japan to allow American merchant ships to use a number of Japanese ports and enabled the creation of an American consulate in Japan. Soon, other western nations demanded the same treatment.

This influx of foreign trade led to the appearance of an anti-foreigner movement in Japan, the *sonnō jōi* ("Revere the Emperor, expel the barbarians"), which, in turn, led to attacks on foreigners and to retaliatory shelling of Japanese towns by western warships. Another group in Japan, led by members of the Satsuma and Chōshū clans, took an entirely different view. They believed that Japan could only prosper and grow if it was to increase contact with the west and appropriate western technologies and concepts.

In early 1867, Emperor Kōmei died and was replaced by his son, the 15-year-old Crown Prince Mutsuhito. One year later, members of the Satsuma-Chōshū alliance attacked and seized the imperial palace in Kyoto. The following day, the young emperor was persuaded to declare the restoration of full imperial power—an event that became known as the Meiji Restoration. This shifting of political power from the shogun to the emperor in 1868 is viewed by many as the official beginning of the Japanese Empire.

Chapter One

The Meiji Restoration

"Virtue is not knowing but doing."

—Japanese proverb

The naming of Japanese emperors can seem confusing to outsiders. During his reign, each ruler is simply known as "The Emperor." His personal name (Mutsushito, in the case of the emperor who began his reign in 1867) is used as a signature but is never referred to even in official documents. In the modern era, it became traditional for each emperor to give the period of his reign a name known as the *nengō* ("era name"). This name was generally used only after the death of the emperor to refer both to that emperor and to the era in which he reigned. After Mutsushito's death, he became known as Meiji (meaning "enlightened rule"), and the period of his rule became known as the Meiji era.

At any rate, after Emperor Meiji and his supporters announced the dissolution of the

Tokugawa Shogunate, they faced opposition from Tokugawa supporters. The conflict that erupted between the two factions became known as the Boshin War, and on January 27, 1868, the two sides confronted one another at the Battle of Toba-Fushimi. This battle also marked a clash of ideologies.

Although the Tokugawa army outnumbered that of the Satsuma-Chōshū alliance by more than three to one, the Tokugawa army retained the traditional means of warfare used by Japanese troops for hundreds of years and had troops armed with swords, pikes, and bows. The army of the Satsuma-Chōshū alliance had embraced western military technology and, while smaller, was armed with new weapons, including one Gatling gun (an early, hand-cranked machine gun), howitzers, and Minie rifles. The outcome of this unequal battle saw the complete defeat of Tokugawa forces, the collapse of the Shogunate, and the surrender of the last main Tokugawa outpost at the castle in Osaka.

As soon as the Boshin War was won, the new rulers of Japan began to enact rapid and far-reaching change. Envoys were dispatched around the world to renegotiate the one-sided agreements imposed on Japan following the Kanagawa Treaty. Japanese observers were sent to Europe and America to observe the industrialization happening there and to learn how Japanese industry could be updated. Western experts were brought to Japan to share their knowledge.

The new rule also began to change the rigid feudal caste system that had been in effect in Japan throughout the Tokugawa Shogunate. The samurai armies maintained by each domain in Japan were abolished in 1872, and a new national army was created. The traditional and hereditary right of samurai to wear their swords at all times was repealed. The lowest caste of *burakumin*—those who worked as undertakers, butchers, tanners, and other occupations considered to involve *kegare* ("defilement")— was abolished.

Not everyone was happy with these reforms or the speed with which they were enacted. Beginning in 1873, there were a number of rebellions by samurai who objected violently to what they saw as the undermining of their prestige within Japanese society. Many samurai refused to accept the introduction of mandatory military conscription for all male citizens of Japan in 1871. Previously, only samurai could be warriors, but these new laws (called by some Japanese the "blood tax") seemed to suggest that any Japanese citizen could be trained to become a soldier. As a result, a series of uprisings against the new government broke out. These were brutally suppressed, and up to 60,000 people were arrested or executed.

The fiercest challenge to the new emperor and the new system of rule came, ironically, from the Satsuma domain, one of the first supporters of the Meiji Restoration. A large samurai army under the command of Saigō Takamori rose in rebellion in 1877, leading to the Battle of Tabaruzaka in March, where around 15,000 traditional samurai met a brigade of men of the new Imperial Japanese Army in battle. In truth, the outcome was never really in doubt. The samurai were defeated, Saigō was killed, and the influence of the samurai class, previously such an important factor in Japanese society and politics, was effectively ended. The Battle of Tabaruzaka represented the last organized attempt to oppose the Meiji Restoration, and after 1877, Japan was free to focus on modernization and industrialization.

In the early stages of the Meiji era, Japan also asserted control and governance over the Nanpō, Ryukyu, and Kuril Islands. Still, these moves did not constitute the beginning of a true overseas empire. These islands had traditionally belonged to Japan, and this was simply the reassertion of control in these areas. It would take a war with China to see the beginning of the first real expansion of the Japanese Empire.

Chapter Two

War with China and the Annexation of Korea

"All men are brothers, like the seas throughout the world; so why do winds and waves clash so fiercely everywhere?"

—Emperor Meiji

From its beginning, Emperor Meiji embraced the concept of a market economy and free enterprise capitalism, things that were entirely new to Japan. At first, the Meiji administration built model factories and provided direct subsidies to Japanese companies, encouraging them to study and copy modern methods of production. A new cabal of companies, the *zaibatsu* ("business clique"), became increasingly powerful and influential in Japan's industrialization. The *zaibatsu* included the formation of large companies such as Mitsui and Mitsubishi, which continue to operate to the present day.

Gradually, Japan began to change, becoming a major importer of raw materials and a significant exporter of finished goods, particularly textiles. A new unified currency, the yen, was introduced, and the government also oversaw the creation of a written constitution, a stock market, the introduction of a western-style taxation system, and improvements in the education system. Railroads were built, and new factories producing cotton and silk operated 24 hours a day. All these reforms were undertaken with the express purpose of turning Japan from a feudal, mainly agrarian nation into a modern industrial power.

Progress was slow but steady. By 1900, agriculture still employed 65% of all Japanese workers, but it accounted for just 38% of GDP, with industry employing fewer people but making a significant contribution to GDP. However, Japan's efforts to industrialize were hampered by a lack of raw materials, a factor that would exert a significant influence on the Japanese Empire from its creation.

Virtually all raw materials, including the fuel and iron needed to keep new Japanese factories running, had to be imported from other countries, which left Japan vulnerable to foreign influence. This, in turn, led to Japan considering how it might expand the territory it controlled in order to safeguard supplies of raw materials. The Korean Peninsula, just 30 miles (50 kilometers) north of the Japanese island of Tsushima, was an obvious source of potential expansion for Japan. Korea had abundant natural resources, including coal, iron ore, copper, and timber, all things badly needed to support the growing Japanese industry.

Korea had traditionally been a tributary state of the Chinese Qing dynasty. However, toward the end of the nineteenth century, the Qing dynasty had been weakened by several unsuccessful wars against other nations, and its grip on Korea was less secure. Thus, in 1876, Japan was able to force Korea to sign the Japan-Korea Treaty, assuring Japan of a flow of raw materials from Korea.

In 1894, Korea requested help from the Qing dynasty to suppress an internal rebellion. More than 2,500 Chinese troops arrived in Korea, and in response, Japan sent 8,000 troops to the same area. This situation rapidly led to war between China and Japan. After less than a year, Japan emerged victorious from what became known as the First Sino-Japanese War. Japan not only forced the Chinese to leave Korea but also defeated Chinese armies in the Liaodong Peninsula and virtually destroyed the Chinese navy in the Battle of the Yalu River. The war ended with the signing of the Treaty of Shimonoseki, which guaranteed Japanese influence in Korea and ceded both the Liaodong Peninsula and the island of Taiwan to Japan.

Within Japan, this victory was greeted with euphoria, and it seemed to mark the beginning of a Japanese overseas empire, but that feeling quickly turned to bitterness when western nations, concerned at Japan's growing influence in the region, intervened to rewrite the treaty. Russia, France, and Germany all insisted that Japanese forces leave the Liaodong Peninsula. Japan lacked the military power to take on three of the most powerful nations in Europe and reluctantly agreed. This intervention caused a great deal of anger in Japan, which was further increased when Russia took control of parts of the Liaodong Peninsula and created an important naval base at Port Arthur, the first warm-water port giving Russia year-round access to the Pacific Ocean.

Japan wasn't the only one that was concerned about Russian expansion in Asia. The British, too, were worried about the prospect of Russian warships in the Pacific, and in 1902, Britain and Japan signed the Anglo-Japanese Alliance. This treaty included clauses that each side would remain neutral if the other became involved in a war with another power and also assured active military support in the event of a war with more than one power. This, from the Japanese perspective, was vital; it meant that if Japan were to go to war with Russia, no other great power could intervene without bringing Britain into the war on Japan's side.

In the early years of the twentieth century, a conflict between Japan and the Russian Empire looked increasingly likely, as Russia refused to accept Japanese influence in Korea and continued to expand its naval base in Port Arthur. If such a conflict was to occur, however, most people assumed that Japan would quickly be defeated. After all, Japan had only emerged from feudalism 30 years before, the Russian army was the largest in the world, and the Russian navy was far larger than the Japanese navy, though it was divided amongst the Baltic, Port Arthur, and Vladivostok in the far east.

The Russo-Japanese War finally began in 1904 with a surprise Japanese attack on the Russian fleet in Port Arthur. On land and at sea, Japanese forces proved to be better led and organized than their Russian opponents, and Russia suffered defeat after defeat until the final destruction of a combined Russian fleet at the Battle of Tsushima in 1905. The war ended with the Treaty of Portsmouth in 1905, in which Russia was forced to cede part of Sakhalin Island to Japan. Later that same year, Japan announced that Korea was a Japanese protectorate, and in 1910, it formally annexed the whole Korean Peninsula to Japan.

In only a little over 40 years following the Meiji Restoration, Japan had transformed itself into a modern industrial power with a formidable, well-equipped national army and navy. Acquisitions in Korea and Manchuria had helped to assure Japan of vital sources of raw materials to allow it to continue its expansion and modernization. The Japanese Empire had been created and was already a significant new power in Asia. It had also shown itself capable of fighting and winning a war not just against China but also against a major European empire.

Still, many Japanese people were unhappy. The Japanese economy was close to bankruptcy following the Russo-Japanese War, and the Americans, who had brokered the treaty that ended the war, had refused to agree that the Russian Empire should pay an indemnity to

Japan, something that many Japanese had expected and demanded. Despite the victory it produced, the Russo-Japanese War left many Japanese with a lingering distrust of the western powers and particularly of the United States.

Chapter Three

The Japanese Empire during World War I

"Be not afraid of going slowly, be afraid only of standing still."

—Japanese proverb

In 1912, Emperor Meiji died, and his son, 33-year-old Yoshihito, became the new emperor of Japan. However, Yoshihito, who would become known as Emperor Taishō after his death, was not a healthy man. He had suffered from cerebral meningitis as a very young child, and it is believed that he may also have suffered from lead poisoning in his childhood. Whatever the cause, it was clear that the new emperor had perceptual issues, limited manual dexterity, notable eccentricities, difficulty in maintaining concentration, and that he became tired very easily.

Protocol and decorum governed every element of the emperor's life, and when Emperor Taishō's neurological issues made it difficult for him to follow guidelines, he became seen less and less in public. At the state opening of the Imperial Diet of Japan, observers were horrified to see the emperor apparently pretending to use his rolled-up speech as a telescope to survey the assembly before him. By 1918, Taishō was not considered well enough to undertake even such vital ceremonies as the annual Shinto rituals, the opening of the Diet, or military maneuvers or graduation ceremonies. After 1919, in fact, he was barely seen in public at all.

While Meiji had played an active and direct role in the governance of Japan, the weakness of Taishō marked a significant change in the way in which the country was governed. In particular, the elected representatives of the Upper and Lower Houses that comprised the Imperial Diet assumed direct responsibility for internal and foreign affairs for the first time. For this reason, this period is sometimes referred to as the "Taishō Democracy."

Meanwhile, World War I began in 1914 with the declaration of war by Britain, Russia, and France on Germany and Austria-Hungary. At that time, the Anglo-Japanese Alliance was still in place, and on August 23, Japan entered the war on Britain's side. There was a strong measure of self-interest involved in that decision; Germany had acquired territory in Asia, and it was clear that Japan saw this war as an opportunity to seize this territory while Germany was distracted by fighting in Europe on the Western and Eastern Fronts.

A combined Japanese-British force soon attacked the fortress of Tsingtao, the main naval base of the German East Asia Squadron. By November, the fortress was occupied by Japanese troops, and in other operations, Japan also occupied German territory in China's Shandong Province as well as in German New Guinea and parts of the Caroline, Marianas, and Marshall Islands.

After the fall of the tsarist regime in Russia in 1917, the former Russian Empire was wracked by a bloody civil war between the communist Bolsheviks (the Reds) and those who sought to restore the Russian monarchy (the Whites). Terrified at the potential spread of communism, the Allies sided with the Whites, and Britain, France, and America all sent troops to fight for the Whites in Russia. Before long, U.S. President Woodrow Wilson asked the Japanese government to provide 7,000 troops to serve in an international coalition that would support the American Expeditionary Force in Siberia. Instead, Japan sent 70,000 troops who, by 1918, occupied every major port in Siberia.

Although these Japanese forces were nominally part of an international force sent to support the Whites, they were actually under the direct control of the Japanese government, and it soon became clear that their purpose was not simply to stop the spread of communism but to snatch as much former Russian territory for Japan as possible. For the first time, Britain began to share America's concerns about Japanese territorial ambitions in Asia. The Japanese government thus became subject to intense pressure from both countries, and this, combined with mounting internal protests at the costs of the occupation, finally caused the withdrawal of Japanese troops from Siberia in 1922. By that time, the Anglo-Japanese Alliance had effectively lapsed and was formally ended by Britain in 1923.

Nevertheless, the new League of Nations formalized Japanese occupation of German territory in the Pacific through the so-called Mandate for the German Possessions in the Pacific Ocean Lying North of the Equator. Under the terms of this mandate, German New Guinea became part of the growing Japanese Empire. During the war, Japan had also increased its pressure on China.

In early 1915, the Japanese government delivered to the government of China a document that became known as the "Twenty-One Demands." In return for agreeing not to occupy additional Chinese territory, this document included secret demands that would effectively have turned China into a Japanese protectorate. China published the secret demands, and as a result, both Britain and America applied pressure on Japan to modify its demands. Japan agreed, and it gained relatively little territory in China as a result of World War I.

This incident simply increased the distrust between Japan, America, and Britain. Japan came to see both countries as blocking it from adding territory to its empire, while in Britain and America, there were growing fears about the scale of aggressive Japanese expansion. Before long, former allies would see themselves fighting a new global war on opposing sides.

Chapter Four

Kōdōha: Rise of Militarism and Nationalism

"It was not clear to me that our course was unjustified."

—Emperor Hirohito

Due to concerns over the increasingly obvious illness and weakness of Emperor Taishō, in 1916, his son, Hirohito, was named heir apparent. Increasingly, the young crown prince began to take on many of the duties normally fulfilled by the emperor. In November 1921, Hirohito was proclaimed *Sesshō* ("regent") and took on even more of his father's role. In 1926, when Taishō died, Hirohito formally became emperor of Japan (and would become known as Emperor Shōwa after his death).

From the beginning of his reign, it was clear that Japan was going through fundamental changes that would shape the empire in its final 20 years. Although Japan was nominally a parliamentary democracy, the truth was that power was shared between parliament and a bewildering array of clubs, associations, and secret societies. Within both the Japanese army and navy, secret societies were prevalent, and their members sought to influence the government and foreign and domestic policy. For example, in 1921, U.S. President Warren Harding called a naval conference that was to be held in Washington.

The purpose of the conference was to try to limit a potential naval arms race by agreeing on a maximum permitted size of the fleets of all major nations. The outcome was the Washington Naval Treaty of 1922 which fixed the respective sizes of the fleets of Britain, the United States, France, Italy, and Japan. Although Japan was a signatory to the treaty, it sharply divided opinion both within the Imperial Japanese Navy and amongst the Japanese public. Within the navy, two secret societies were formed as a result: the Treaty Faction (whose members supported the treaty) and the Fleet Faction (whose members were bitterly opposed to the treaty).

Within the Imperial Japanese Army, there were similar divisions supported by rival groups. The moderate *Tōseiha* (Control Faction) was opposed by the *Kōdōha* (Imperial Way Faction), which sought an aggressive expansion of the empire and the creation of a Japanese government controlled by the military. The leader of the Kōdōha, Sadao Araki, a general in the army, also became one of the most influential militaristic thinkers in Japan. Araki made a direct link between the traditional Japanese code of *bushido* (a moral and behavioral code developed by and for samurai warriors) and the growing fascist and nationalistic political movements in Europe.

Starting in 1931, Araki began speaking openly about Kōdōha and its philosophy which stressed the inherent superiority of Japanese culture over all others, the importance of spiritual purity over material possessions, and the need for Japan to attack the Soviet Union and prevent the spread of communism. It also strongly suggested that parliamentary democracy itself was somehow "un-Japanese" and that only the creation of some form of military dictatorship could restore Japan to its rightful place in the world. While Araki was minister of war, this philosophy became prevalent in both the

Japanese army and navy. However, in 1934, one of the principal supporters of the opposing faction, General Hideki Tojo, replaced Araki as war minister, and the navy and army moved toward the more moderate Tōseiha faction.

Unsurprisingly, the activities of these rival factions brought turmoil and chaos to the government of Japan. Those who favored militarism gained additional support when the effects of the Great Depression began to be felt in Japan. Japan's growing population (close to 65 million in 1930), combined with a shortage of agricultural land, meant that Japan had to import food. However, the depression, combined with trade tariffs in many other countries, inhibited Japan's ability to export. Militarists such as those in the Kōdōha argued that Japan could only thrive through the development of an army and navy sufficiently powerful to impose its will by force. The only thing that the ultranationalists debated was the direction of Japan's expansion: should it attack China or the Soviet Union?

The rivalry of competing factions in Japan was instrumental in creating a situation where relatively small groups could have a disproportionate impact on the policy of successive governments. When violent, militaristic, ultranationalist factions came to dominate the navy and army in the late 1930s, this had a huge impact on Japanese foreign policy and led directly to Japan's involvement in World War II.

Chapter Five

Manchuria and the Kwantung Army

"Japan will oppose any attempt at international control of Manchuria. It does not mean that we defy you, because Manchuria belongs to us by right."

—Yosuke Matsuoka, Japanese Delegate to the League of Nations

The region of northeast China known as Manchuria was an important factor in Japanese foreign policy following World War I. Manchuria borders northern Korea (which the Japanese controlled after 1910) as well as Russia to the north. In order to protect Korea from potential invasion from China, Japan had negotiated a series of treaties that assured the area's neutrality as well as provided Japan with important mining concessions. However, developments in China began to raise concerns in Japan about the security of this region.

In 1912, the Republic of China was created following the Xinhai Revolution, which overthrew the Qing dynasty. The creation of the republic also led to the rise of a number of local warlords who fought for domination of areas of China. This fragmentation and division of power were to Japan's advantage, as no single faction in China was sufficiently strong to challenge the Japanese army and navy. It was not until 1928 that the country achieved a level of unification under the rule of General Chiang Kai-shek. A bloody civil war with the remaining warlords from 1928 to 1930 further increased the area controlled by Chiang Kai-shek, but China was far from a single, unified nation even after the end of the warlord era in 1930.

The internal wars that had affected China for most of the first three decades of the twentieth century prevented large-scale industrialization and ensured that its economy remained largely stagnant. Still, many people in Japan viewed the control exerted by China over Manchuria as a direct threat to Japanese interests in that area and in Korea. From the north, too, Manchuria faced a growing threat from the increasing military power of the Soviet Union.

Following its victory in the Russo-Japanese War in 1905, Japan had been granted control over the China Far East Railway in Manchuria, which included over 1,000 miles (1,600 kilometers) of track that connected all major towns and cities in the region. Japan had also been given control over what became known as the South Manchuria Railway Zone, an area extending for more than 30 miles (50 kilometers) on either side of all sections of this railway, and had the right to station guards in this territory to protect the railroad. Under the same treaty, Japan was allowed to station troops in the Kwantung Leased Territory, part of the Liaodong Peninsula originally leased to Japan by China in 1895. After World War I, the Japanese army stationed in Manchuria and Liaodong Peninsula became known as the Kwantung Army. Nominally, the role of this army was simply to guard and protect territory near Japanese bases and adjacent to the China Far East Railway, but soon it expanded to become the most important and most prestigious command within the Imperial Japanese Army.

By the early 1930s, the Kwantung Army had grown to become the most powerful army in Asia. It had also become a hotbed of the Kōdōha faction, and its members advocated the seizure of territory by force, particularly territory in

Manchuria. Although the Kwantung Army was nominally under the control of the Japanese High Command and therefore also of the Japanese government, it began to act unilaterally and without consideration of orders from home. Acting against the official Japanese policy of non-intervention in China, the Kwantung Army became secretly involved in local conflicts with a number of Chinese warlords throughout the 1920s.

Then, on the night of September 18, 1931, a small explosion damaged a section of the China Far East Railway near the city of Mukden. The explosion caused little serious damage, and it is now widely believed to have been caused by members of the Kwantung Army who wished to create a justification for a Japanese occupation of all of Manchuria. Within three months, Japanese troops of the Kwantung Army, acting without orders or permission from the government or army High Command, occupied large areas of Chinese Manchuria. When the government issued orders that the invasion was to cease and Japanese troops were to return to their barracks, the orders were simply ignored.

The Chinese leader, General Chiang Kai-shek, already battling resistance in other parts of China, ordered Chinese troops in Manchuria to withdraw and instead appealed to the League of Nations to intervene. An international commission identified Japan as the aggressor and demanded that Japanese troops withdraw. The Japanese government refused to do this (and it lacked the control over the Kwantung Army to make it happen anyway), and as a direct result, Japan withdrew from the League of Nations, increasing its international isolation.

In 1932, Manchukuo (Japanese-controlled Manchuria) was proclaimed an independent state, but its supposed independence was doubted by most other nations, and very few formally recognized its existence. Although the Japanese invasion of Manchuria significantly expanded the Japanese Empire, it led Japan inexorably into conflict with other powers, and it is astonishing to consider that it was carried out not on the orders of the Japanese government or military High Command but instead by a renegade army inspired by the precepts of Kōdōha.

Chapter Six

Coups and Political Violence

"Asia for the Asians."

—Japanese slogan

During the late 1920s and the 1930s, the actions of some army and Japanese navy officers became increasingly violent and aimed at replacing the civilian administration with some form of military rule. Successive governments seemed powerless to curtail this violence. Members of the Kwantung Army had murdered a Chinese warlord, Chang Tso-lin, in 1929, but neither the Diet nor the military High Command seemed willing to risk pressing for the identification and arrest of those responsible. The government fell as a result, and the prime minister of the succeeding government, Hamaguchi Osachi, was assassinated by a young nationalist supporter in

1930 when he attempted to curtail the power of the Japanese military.

After the Japanese occupation of Manchuria, a new government was formed in December 1931, led by Prime Minister Inukai Tsuyoshi. Inukai was completely opposed to the growing power of the military and attempted to curtail further military advances in Manchuria and planned to send a Japanese envoy to China to negotiate the withdrawal of Japanese troops in the area. In May 1932, after just six months in office, Inukai was murdered by a group of ultranationalist officers from the Imperial Japanese Army.

Political murder became almost commonplace, with not just politicians but prominent business leaders being killed by various military factions. The Japanese army announced that it would no longer take orders from any party cabinet, and anyone voicing opposition to the army or navy risked attack or assassination. In an effort to restore order, a retired admiral of the navy, Saitō Makoto, was appointed prime minister. Yet even this did not appease the followers of Kōdōha.

In February 1936, military members of the Kōdōha faction attempted a coup. Saitō Makoto and several leading political figures were assassinated, and the plotters were able to seize control of many government buildings in Tokyo, but critically, not the imperial palace. Emperor Hirohito soon made clear his displeasure at this latest attempt at the military to take power. Faced with the condemnation of the emperor, the remainder of the army felt it had no choice but to act against the rebels. Government buildings were retaken, and the leaders of the rebellion were rounded up, tried, and quickly executed. Supporters of the Kōdōha faction were removed from senior military positions and were replaced by members of the more moderate Tōseiha faction.

While political violence diminished following the failed coup in 1936, even members of the Tōseiha were dedicated to expanding the Japanese Empire. All were committed to the creation of a "New Order" in Asia that would see the colonial possessions of European nations replaced by what would later become known as the Greater East Asia Co-Prosperity Sphere, a new confederation of Asian states controlled by Japan. In Asia, there was growing feeling against colonial rule, and the creation by Japan of what appeared to be a pan-Asian group that supported independence and freedom found many supporters in other countries. Only too late would those countries understand that this new group simply replaced colonial rule with rule by Japan.

To most people in Japan and elsewhere, it had come to seem inevitable that the Japanese Empire would soon find itself at war with the European colonial powers and possibly also with the United States. Thus, personnel and equipment were poured into Manchuria to extract its natural resources as quickly as possible in order to enable Japanese industry to support massive rearmament. The road toward global war was also made more likely as Japan grew closer to two belligerent nations in Europe: Germany and Italy.

Chapter Seven

Alliance with Germany and Italy

"Japan, Germany, and Italy agree to . . . undertake to assist one another with all political, economic, and military means."

—The Tripartite Pact

In 1937, a dispute between Japanese and Chinese troops in Beijing led to the outbreak of a full-scale war between Japan and China. Some historians mark this as the true beginning of World War II, though others suggest that it began as early as 1931 with the Japanese invasion of Manchuria. Whatever the case, the Second Sino-Japanese War would continue until 1945 and would claim the lives of up to 25 million Chinese people through conflict, famine, and disease. Some people have gone as far as to call it the "Asian holocaust."

Initially, Japanese troops won a number of significant victories, quickly taking the cities of Nanjing, Shanghai, and Beijing. However, the Japanese were unable to completely defeat the Chinese Nationalist Army, and after the establishment of the Sino-Soviet Treaty in 1937, the Soviet Union began to supply the Chinese with weapons and aircraft. Japan found itself involved in a long war that would prove to be a constant drain on resources and personnel. Many Japanese saw the support provided by the Soviet Union as a significant factor in prolonging this war, and this simply increased Japanese fears of the Soviet Union and the spread of communism, which many saw as the antithesis of traditional Japanese values. Thus, Japan began to look for allies.

In Europe at this time, there was only one power bloc that was implacably opposed to communism: Nazi Germany and fascist Italy. In Germany, Hitler had come to power in 1933, and he had long been vocal in his opposition to communism in general and the Soviet Union in particular. In November 1936, Japan and Germany signed the Agreement against the Communist International (widely called the Anti-Comintern Pact, which Italy also joined in 1937), ostensibly an agreement by both to oppose communism, but in reality, an agreement to oppose further expansion of the Soviet Union. Many people in Japan and Germany saw parallels between the growth of nationalism and militarism in both countries, and these common ideologies seemed to provide the basis for an alliance of some sort.

However, the Anti-Comintern Pact proved to be short-lived. Hitler was determined to expand German territory to the east, into Czechoslovakia and Poland. He knew that this might involve war with France and Britain, and he needed to be certain that it would not also involve the Soviet Union; German military power was not strong enough to fight a war on two fronts against three powerful enemies simultaneously. Although he privately remained committed to the destruction of the Soviet Union, Hitler encouraged the creation in 1939 of the Molotov-Ribbentrop Pact, a non-aggression treaty between Germany and the Soviet Union that would ensure Russia's neutrality if Germany invaded Poland. The signature of this pact caused a distinct cooling in relations between Japan and Germany.

Just one month after concluding this treaty with the Soviet Union, Germany went to war with Britain and France. Within less than one year and following a series of rapid military campaigns, Germany controlled most of mainland Europe. Once again, Hitler began to turn his attention to the east. In September 1940, Germany, Italy, and Japan signed a new agreement, the Tripartite Pact, a defensive alliance between the three nations. Though this pact still considered the Soviet Union, its main focus was America, which Japan was coming to see as the main barrier to the continued expansion of the Japanese Empire.

In America, public opinion had turned against Japan following the outbreak of the Second Sino-Japanese War in 1937. Newspaper accounts of atrocities committed by Japanese troops contributed to this view, particularly the news of large-scale massacres of Chinese civilians carried out after the capture of Nanjing. This was made even worse in December 1937 when Japanese aircraft attacked several U.S. ships attempting to evacuate Americans from Nanjing, though the Japanese formally apologized, claiming that the attack had been a mistake.

In 1940, the administration of President Franklin D. Roosevelt began to harden its attitude toward Japan in response to continued Japanese attacks against China and the signature of the Tripartite Pact. Although the U.S. was not directly involved in World War II yet, it viewed the fascist states of Germany and Italy as a threat to its interests, and by aligning itself with these nations, Japan was also increasingly seen as a direct threat to America.

In early 1940, America began to formally provide aid to China and to place embargoes on the export of goods to Japan that would be used for military purposes. This, in turn, presented a major threat to Japan's ability to continue to build up its armed forces. Imports from America of iron ore and steel were critical to Japanese industry, and oil from the U.S. was vital to keep Japanese aircraft, ships, and tanks operational. The United States refused to lift this embargo unless Japanese troops withdrew from China— something that the Japanese government refused even to consider.

Japan was faced with what it saw as a stark choice. Without imports from America, it could not hope to continue the war in China for long. However, some Japanese began to believe that there was another alternative: a rapid, aggressive war against America during which Japan could occupy territory that would provide the oil, iron ore, and steel it desperately needed to maintain its empire. A plan was set in motion, one which would see the Japanese strike American soil and force the world power into World War II.

Chapter Eight

World War II: Pearl Harbor

"The fate of the Empire rests on this enterprise. Every man must devote himself totally to the task in hand."

—Admiral Isoroku Yamamoto

By 1941, the war with China was not going as planned for Japan. Even in areas that were nominally conquered, continuing guerilla attacks targeted Japanese troops and installations. These led to savage reprisal, which, in turn, persuaded more Chinese to turn against their Japanese occupiers. More than half of the total Imperial Japanese Army and Air Force was directly involved in the war in China, and there was no prospect of the war ending in the immediate future.

Japan began to look to other areas in the region for expansion that would provide the raw materials needed to make Japan self-sufficient. The Netherlands and France had both been defeated by Nazi Germany, but both still held important colonial assets in Asia, including the Dutch East Indies (present-day Indonesia) and French Indochina (present-day Vietnam). The British, still fighting Germany and Italy, also had colonies in Hong Kong, Burma, Singapore, and the Malay Peninsula. If Japan could seize these territories, it would have access to the oil and other raw materials it so badly needed. However, it was clear that any aggressive Japanese toward these colonial territories would almost certainly lead to war with America.

In secret, the Japanese High Command developed a strategy for fighting a war many saw as inevitable. A bold tactical plan was developed by the commander-in-chief of the Japanese Combined Fleet, Admiral Yamamoto Isoroku. Japanese aircraft would launch a surprise attack on the U.S. Pacific Fleet at Pearl Harbor. This would buy time for other Japanese forces to rapidly occupy Dutch and British colonial holdings in the region. The Japanese Empire would be expanded so that it would extend from Burma in the west to the Dutch East Indies and northern New Guinea in the south and to the Marshall and Gilbert Islands in the east. Japanese military leaders believed they could successfully defend this new perimeter against any potential British or American attacks. Faced with the reality of an expanded and now self-sufficient Japanese Empire, it was hoped that Britain and America would then be forced to sue for peace.

In accordance with this plan, on December 7, 1941, Japanese aircraft operating from four aircraft carriers attacked the U.S. Pacific Fleet at Pearl Harbor. To ensure surprise, this attack was carried out without a declaration of war. The attack on Pearl Harbor did indeed catch the Americans off-guard; eight battleships were badly damaged, many smaller vessels were sunk, almost two hundred aircraft were destroyed, and over two thousand servicemen were killed. The Japanese lost only a handful of aircraft in the attack and a little over sixty men. Before the attack on Pearl Harbor, Admiral Yamamoto had promised that during the first six months of war with Britain and America, "I will run wild and win victory upon victory." He was quickly proved to be absolutely correct.

On December 25, British-controlled Hong Kong fell to the Japanese. By early February 1942, Japanese troops occupied all of the Malay Peninsula and the vital British base in Singapore. Three months later, Japanese troops occupied the

American-controlled Philippines and large parts of British Burma. Japan had achieved the first part of its plan, the establishment of a new perimeter for the Japanese Empire and the acquisition of raw materials. The only thing that remained to be seen was whether, as planned, they could successfully defend this perimeter against Allied attacks.

In some former colonial possessions, the Japanese were initially welcomed and regarded, at least partly, as liberators who were working toward the creation of a new pan-Asian power bloc. However, the brutality of the occupation in many areas soon changed perceptions of the Japanese, who became regarded as occupiers who were just as intent on exploiting local people and resources as the colonial powers had ever been. As resistance to the Japanese occupation grew, larger and larger numbers of Japanese troops were needed to maintain order, leaving Japanese military resources stretched very thin.

The Japanese strategic plan also contained a fundamental flaw. It was predicated on a short, victorious war after which America would rapidly seek peace terms. This was necessary for Japan: the U.S. population and industrial capacity were much greater than Japan's, and

America could produce weapons, aircraft, tanks, and ships far more rapidly than Japan. It had also become apparent following the Japanese attack on Pearl Harbor and during other actions in the early war in the Pacific that air power had become a vital new factor, and aircraft carriers had become the most important warships. Although the attack on Pearl Harbor had generally been a success, by chance, the three carriers of the U.S. Pacific Fleet had been at sea and had escaped damage. These ships would be an important factor in the battles to come, and America could produce four new carriers for every one that Japan could produce.

To the horror of many senior Japanese military leaders, the United States did not seek peace terms after the initial Japanese success in the Pacific. Instead, it accepted the need for a long war in the Pacific and in Europe against Germany and Italy. The coda to Admiral Yamamoto's confident pre-war statement about running wild for six months was quickly shown to be all too true, "But then, if the war continues after that, I have no expectation of success."

Chapter Nine

The Tide Turns

"The war has developed not necessarily to Japan's advantage."

—Emperor Hirohito

On June 4, 1942, almost precisely six months after the Japanese attack on Pearl Harbor, Japanese and American naval forces met in battle near the island of Midway, in the extreme northwest end of the Hawaiian island chain. The Japanese intended to occupy the island and sent a large invasion force supported by a naval task force that included four aircraft carriers. The U.S. Navy, having broken Japanese secret codes, learned of the attack and sent their own task force to the area that included three aircraft carriers.

The resulting Battle of Midway was one of the first naval engagements fought exclusively between air groups from the carriers involved, with none of the capital ships of either side coming close enough to engage the enemy. The outcome was a stunning victory for the U.S. All four Japanese carriers were sunk, and the majority of Japan's most experienced pilots and aircrew were lost. One notable military historian has called this "the most stunning and decisive blow in the history of naval warfare."

From the time of the attack on Pearl Harbor to the Battle of Midway, the Japanese Empire did not suffer a single notable military defeat. After this battle, it never won a single major victory. After Midway, America switched to the offensive, with a two-pronged assault against the new Japanese perimeter. The U.S. Navy began an "island-hopping" campaign in which one Japanese island after another was the subject of assault by American forces. The first began in August 1942 with an attack on the important Japanese air and naval base on the island of Guadalcanal. As in virtually all subsequent island battles, Japanese resistance was tenacious, and casualties on both sides were very high during six months of bitter fighting, but inexorably, Japanese-occupied islands were taken and turned into Allied bases.

In Papua New Guinea, U.S. Army forces under the command of General Douglas MacArthur advanced against Japanese resistance, and by March 1943, they had crushed the Japanese defense and isolated the vital Japanese base at Rabaul. MacArthur's troops continued their progress toward the Dutch East Indies and the Philippines while the navy launched another amphibious assault on the Japanese-held island of Tarawa. It was clear that the Japanese plan to defend the perimeter of their expanded empire was doomed to fail. The limited military capacity of the empire was simply too small to protect the vast new territory it had conquered. Still, within Japan, there was no consideration of surrender or even of pursuing peace talks with the United States.

By early 1944, most of the southwest Pacific was in American hands, and within a few months, the U.S. Army and Navy had also occupied former Japanese strongholds in the Marshall and Mariana island chains. These were particularly important because, from airbases on those islands, a new American long-range bomber, the B-29 Superfortress, could launch bombing attacks on the Japanese home islands. Starting in June 1944, American raids on Japan killed over 300,000 Japanese civilians and severely curtailed Japanese industrial production.

In April 1945, U.S. forces began an assault on the smallest and least populated of the five main islands that comprised Japan: Okinawa. This was the largest amphibious assault in history, and its cost in human terms was horrendous. Over 14,000 U.S. troops, 75,000 Japanese troops, and more than 100,000 civilians died during the 82-day battle for the island. The outcome was an American victory, but many feared the cost of mounting an assault on any of the other Japanese home islands. The new U.S. president, Harry Truman, was horrified at the casualties on Okinawa and feared the cost of subsequent planned invasions of Kyushu and Honshu. The strategic bombing of Japan was clearly causing large-scale civilian casualties and damaging Japanese factories, but there were no signs that Japan was ready to surrender.

Within the Japanese Empire, there was a growing recognition that the war could not be won, but the only viable strategy seemed to be a defense of all territory so implacable that high casualties might force the U.S. to offer Japan an "honorable" peace. Then, on August 9, Russia declared war on Japan, and Russian forces attacked the Japanese Kwantung Army in Manchuria. Japan was now facing a war on two fronts that it could not hope to win, but still, most Japanese military leaders would not countenance any consideration of surrender.

It would take the use of a new and horrifying weapon to finally force the Japanese Empire to surrender. By July 1945, the top-secret Manhattan Project had led to the creation of two nuclear weapons—one using plutonium and the other uranium. A small atomic bomb had been tested in America, so the concept was known to be viable, but no one really knew what would happen if nuclear weapons were to be dropped on heavily populated cities. On July 26, Allied leaders issued the Potsdam Declaration, which stated that unless Japan surrendered immediately and unconditionally, Allied bombing attacks would lead to the "inevitable and complete destruction of the Japanese armed forces and just as inevitably the utter devastation of the Japanese homeland."

The Japanese government ignored this statement and noted only that Japan would continue to fight "until the end." Thus, on August 6, an American bomber named *Enola Gay* dropped a nuclear weapon on the city of Hiroshima. President Truman issued a statement to Japan noting that "if they do not now accept our terms, they may expect a rain of ruin from the air, the like of which has never been seen on this earth." Still, the Japanese leadership made no move toward surrender.

On August 9, a second nuclear weapon was dropped on the city of Nagasaki. The effects of the use of nuclear weapons on two Japanese cities were devastating. Somewhere in the region of 200,000 civilians died either as a direct result of the bombing or were killed by the effects of radiation poisoning. Emperor Hirohito now made it clear that Japan had no choice but to surrender. However, there was one last attempt by Japanese soldiers to prevent this. When they learned that the emperor intended to broadcast a message announcing Japan's surrender on August 15, officers from the Staff Office of the Ministry of War of Japan and the Imperial Guard attempted to stage a coup in order to continue the war. They murdered senior officers and attempted to occupy the imperial palace and place Hirohito under arrest. They failed, and all those involved in the attempted coup committed ritual suicide. World War II was finally over.

Chapter Ten

End of the Empire

"We are resolved to endure the unendurable and suffer what is not sufferable."

—Emperor Hirohito

On August 15, 1945, Emperor Hirohito made a radio broadcast in which he announced that Japan was prepared to surrender. The emperor noted that "We declared war on America and Britain out of our sincere desire to ensure Japan's self-preservation and the stabilization of East Asia, it being far from our thought either to infringe upon the sovereignty of other nations or to embark upon territorial aggrandizement." Hirohito also stated that "The enemy has begun to employ a new and most cruel bomb, the power of which to do damage is, indeed, incalculable, taking the toll of many innocent lives." The statement concluded by warning Japanese people to "beware most strictly of any outbursts of emotion which may engender needless complications."

Shortly after, almost one million Allied troops under the command of General Douglas MacArthur occupied the Japanese home islands. Japanese troops were withdrawn from Korea, Manchuria, and all other territories they had occupied. Russian troops meanwhile invaded and occupied southern Sakhalin Island, which had been ceded to Japan after the Russo-Japanese War in 1905. With these losses, the Japanese Empire ceased to exist.

Following MacArthur's guidance, the Japanese government enacted sweeping new laws that brought true parliamentary democracy to Japan for the first time, dissolved all of Japan's armed forces, and severely curtailed the power of the emperor. A new constitution, written partly by the American military, was enacted in 1947 and became the basis for the modern nation of Japan. The new constitution and the new laws demanded by the Americans were intended not just to mark the final end of the Japanese Empire but also to ensure that Japan could never again begin to build such an empire.

The American occupation, and direct American control over the civil administration of Japan, ended in 1951 with the signature of the

San Francisco Peace Treaty. However, under the terms of the Treaty of Mutual Cooperation and Security between the United States and Japan, also signed in 1951, America retained the right to station tens of thousands of troops in Japan.

By that time, the United States faced a new potential enemy: the Soviet Union. What would become known as the Cold War—a series of confrontations between America and Russia and their allies—would change American attitudes toward Japan. In the first phases of the American occupation, the prime motivation had been a desire to punish Japan for the war in the Pacific and to ensure that it would never again be strong enough to threaten military action. Yet as the Cold War intensified, Americans began to see Japan as an important potential ally against the Soviet Union. Efforts were made to help Japan restore its economy and to once again become an independent nation. Before long, Japan came to be seen as an Asian stronghold of democracy and capitalism and one of America's most important allies in the region.

Conclusion

At its peak, the Japanese Empire covered more than 3 million square miles (8.5 million square kilometers) and governed 450 million people, over 20% of the population of the Earth at that time. This was one of the largest empires in world history. One of the most notable aspects of the empire was the stunning rapidity with which it was created.

Prior to 1870, Japan had been a largely agrarian country with a feudal system of government and control. In just a few decades following the Meiji Restoration, Japan transformed itself into a modern, industrial nation with a well-equipped and well-trained army and navy. The power of Japan's military forces was graphically demonstrated in two victorious wars—first against China and then against the Russian Empire. These wars led to the creation of an overseas empire but also to a feeling amongst some Japanese people that Japan was not being given its due rewards and was perhaps being deliberately constrained by European powers and the United States.

There was probably some justification for these views. Japan's growing power and influence in Asia were viewed with concern and disquiet in many western countries. Still, it does seem possible that the Japanese Empire might have continued to grow slowly and stably, but for one pivotal moment that changed the subsequent history of the empire and of Asia as a whole: the invasion of Manchuria by the Kwantung Army in 1931.

Ultranationalism—the belief that Japanese culture and society were somehow innately superior to all others and therefore pre-destined to rule other people—infused sections of Japan and was particularly prevalent within the Kwantung Army. To the men of this army, the subjugation of China seemed not just necessary for Japan's continued expansion but a moral duty. It's worth reiterating that this invasion of Manchuria was done without the sanction of the Japanese government or the military High Command. It was unilaterally undertaken by an army that no longer recognized the authority of either and used threats of political violence to ensure that its actions were not challenged within Japan.

Many of the men of the Kwantung Army believed that China would quickly be defeated and occupied. They were wrong. Japan would be compelled to send a large proportion of its military force to fight in Manchuria up to 1945. This weakened Japan's ability to undertake later aggressive military campaigns. Even more serious, the Japanese invasion of Manchuria and particularly news of Japanese atrocities carried out against Chinese civilians hardened international opinion against Japan and led to direct confrontation with both the Soviet Union and America to the point where a war against one or both seemed virtually certain.

An unbroken string of military victories since 1895 had left many Japanese with the view that their armed forces were so intrinsically superior to all others that they could win a war against even the mighty industrial capacity of the United States. For a little over six months, from December 1941 to May 1942, this view seemed to be justified as Japanese forces swept across the Pacific and expanded the Japanese Empire to its greatest extent. However, from the Battle of Midway on, U.S. troops proved just as dogged and determined as their Japanese counterparts. Slowly but surely, the Japanese Empire was forced back until the bombings of Hiroshima and Nagasaki finally ended the Second World War.

The war in the Pacific killed somewhere in the region of 25 million people, with only 6 million of those being combatants, mostly

Chinese and Japanese. This war shaped the course of subsequent Asian history. It led to the creation of independence movements that, within 30 years of the end of the war, would see most former colonial possessions in Asia achieving independence. Japan, meanwhile, became one of the most powerful and successful economies not only in Asia but in the world.

Bibliography

Matsusaka, Y. T. (2003). *The Making of Japanese Manchuria, 1904-1932.*

Paine, S. C. M. (2017). *The Japanese Empire: Grand Strategy from the Meiji Restoration to the Pacific War.*

Yellen, J. A. (2019). *The Greater East Asia Co-Prosperity Sphere: When Total Empire Met Total War.*

Young, L. (1999). *Japan's Total Empire: Manchuria and the Culture of Wartime Imperialism.*

Printed in Great Britain
by Amazon